MONK CONSPIRACY

Mark Watson

CONTENTS

CHARACTERS

*Majid— head monk

*Fr Bernard— 5th columnist

*Sr Helena — more than a friend to Majid

*Jose — leader of the rebels

*Fr Matthias — poisoned

*Sr Simona— infirmary nurse

*James — household refuge for Majid's friends

*rebel nun who is a man

*Fr Wilson — monk medic

*Fr Brittain — chief scientific monk

*Michael — love child of Majid & Sr Helena

CHAPTER 1

Nestled by the banks of the River Seine lies an incredible abbey and monastery full of Benedictine monks and religious brothers. Originally the order was founded in 529 AD in Italy, and spread throughout Europe and then South America and other parts of the world. Monastic life centres around prayer and working, whether in vineyards or other agricultural pursuits. In the early years it was the main monastic order. The strictness of silence, especially during Mass and mealtimes, is very much adhered to.

The year is 1793 and France is in turmoil. Fighting is going on everywhere; it is the Civil War.

Majid, the monk, is a popular monk at the abbey. He has lots of friends. He is 38 years old.

The day starts with prayers at 4.30am and with a wakeup call at 4.00am, via a knock on the door. Then breakfast is at 7.00am, followed by more prayers, and then Mass at 10.00am.

Then prayers are at 1.00pm, followed by lunch at 1.30 pm, and then prayers again. Not all the monks go to every session as it depends on what they are doing at the monastery at any specific time. After all, they are at a working monastery where they make wine and there are gardens to tend to.

The days are busy, and Majid often carries a bible to church and often holds it for the abbot as he says prayers and Masses. Majid came from Algiers and found that he needed to come to France as he had been persecuted in Algeria. He was born into a Christian family and had heard about the Benedictines from his grandfather, who was a merchant and traded with France regularly. Grandpa talked about France incessantly and all its' great attributes, and he mentioned the Benedictines as they sold wine to him. It was of the highest quality. Majid was enamoured with the French way of life and also, he hankered for a peaceful existence after all the abuse he received because of his Christian beliefs. He studied the Benedictines philosophy and so a monastic life beckoned.

The grounds of this magnificent abbey are flush with blooms amidst all the delightful pathways caressing the property. One could get lost as if one was in another dimension.

There are many buildings, and the first buildings were built in the 11th century. There are a series of buildings sprawled across the centre of the 20-acre property. The main building has six storeys of magnificent stony architecture, and construction began in the 11th century. The side of the building overlooks the river. At the other end is the main church which is where all the priests and brothers pray daily. Besides the main part of the abbey which has an amazing church there is another church adjacent to the front gate. The latter church is where all the lay people come to pray and celebrate Mass. It forms part of the barrier to the outside. The main church has tall internal stone pillars and the clergy sit within the altar area where the priests celebrate mass. There is a small communion rail that separates the congregation from the brothers and priests. Specially invited guests are welcomed into the church at various times and are usually visiting clergy or prominent towns' people. To the east and west of the main buildings are beautiful gardens maintained by several priests. The buildings are grandiose and extensive and were built around 1020. They are resplendent in a dark brown brick. The monastery looks incredibly well preserved despite its 700-year age. It stands out as the main building for many miles and a target in the civil war.

Today one can hear gunshots in the distance, and the sounds of cannon shells exploding making a rumbling sound. The rebels are getting closer.

The high walls of the abbey are an imposing barrier and on the riverside the abbey grounds tower almost 30 ft above the river.

''Gaboom'' then ''splash' 'upriver a mile or so are worrying sounds. The fighting is getting closer. Priests and brothers are targets. Majid hands out guns to his contemporaries.

The walls are tall and thick.

CHAPTER 2

A rebel climbs to the top of the non-riverside wall and he attempts to climb over the barrier, whereupon one of the monks shoots him.

''Kepow'' rings out chillingly around the abbey grounds. Life and death!

Majid hurriedly corrals his fellow monks to guard the walls at strategic points. ''Bang! Bang!' as more shots ring out.

There are some nuns also staying at the abbey,

''Sister, sister'' yells Majid.

''Come this way'' exhorts Majid.

''Follow me'' says Majid.

Majid runs with the nuns to a secret entrance in the gardens.

''Quick! Quick! Follow me down these stairs'' says Majid. Sr Simona is the infirmary nurse and has been very supportive to the wounded monk soldiers. She is always either in church or assisting in the infirmary. Sister Helena is a very erudite lady who has been so supportive to Majid, especially as he came from an impoverished background in Algeria. She is a person who is always willing to help.

They scramble down the narrow spiralling small steps to a door which Majid hurriedly opens.

A tunnel lies ahead descending. The secret passageway is nestled very discreetly in the east gardens. It is almost undetectable. It is quite overgrown with shrubs and very inconspicuous.

'Come on sisters, hurry the rebels are approaching'' shouts Majid.

The dark unlit tunnel is only exposed by Majid's large lit candle.

The monks have been defending this monastery for 700 years and they will not let it be taken. It has been defended at all costs. The monks believe completely in their God and Jesus Christ. Their belief systems are strong. Might is right.

The sisters, in their white regalia, follow obediently onward.

They finally reach the end of the tunnel which exits at the river, and it is fortunately pitch black as night has closed in.

Majid ushers the sisters onto the cart, and jumps on the front and grabs the reins.

''Giddy-up,'' he whispers to the two horses.

Off they canter into the distance to hopefully safe quarters.

Majid has friends on the outside.

The horses travel for half an hour to a nearby village. There await his friends. The village is a typical French 18th century village, resplendent with many stone buildings and narrow streets. Little alleyways crisscross the narrow streets. James, Majid's good friend, lives off one of these alleyways. Majid parks the horses at a meadow close by which has plenty of grass.

Majid knocks on the front door in a carefully programmed sequence to alert his friends inside to who it is.

At the front door comes this chubby affable individual who looks eager to assist.

''Hi, James, please shelter these sisters, would you, as the rebels are advancing on the abbey,'' he pleads. James has been a long-standing friend of Majid, since he came to France from Algeria. They met at the church where he sits adjacent to the monastery many years ago.

James ushers them inside and blows out the large candle as he has a much smaller dimly lit one.

James pronounces, "We can't be too careful."

He continues ''Sisters you will need to get out of those habits pronto. Don't worry, I have clothes for you all.''

The sisters quickly undress and put on new clothes whilst the faint drum of explosions can be heard in the distance.''

At that point Majid whispers, 'I must get back to the abbey to be with my fellow monks and brothers.''

CHAPTER 3

Meanwhile back at the abbey there can be heard more shots as the opportunistic invaders have been repelled, but at cost. Some of the monks have been shot and moved to the main chapel to be attended by the nuns who have had nursing experience.

The remaining depleted monks take it in turns to guard the walls in two shifts. One shift is praying and the other guarding the walls.

"A lull in the fighting for a few days is a blessing, for nothing should breach the walls," the abbot shouts.

Back indoors the monks are going about their lunch in the main hall.

Suddenly one of the monks collapses as Majid appears in the dining room.

''What is wrong with Father Matthias?'' shouts Majid.

He continues, 'He doesn't look at all well.''

As Majid turns him over, he is frothing at the mouth.

''I think he has been poisoned,'' screams Majid.

The other priests and brothers start milling around.

Eventually Fr Matthias takes his last breath, and then some broken gasps, and then nothing. Fr Matthias is dead.

Fr Matthias, in his mid-60's, had been one of the long-standing monastic members of the abbey and had been resident at the monastery since he began training at age 18. Fr Matthias was a jovial character and kept the monastic members upbeat. He was always making jokes and making fellow priests laugh.

Who could have murdered Fr Matthias?'' considers Majid. Majid always looked up to Fr Matthias who had taught him a lot. He was second in charge at the monastery.

The fellow monks carry his body to the makeshift morgue set up since the rebels started attacking, and he was in good company with other dead monks and priests.

''What next?" thought Majid.

There was a fifth columnist at the abbey. "A traitor in our midst," ponders Majid.

''How can we flush him out?'' thinks Majid.

Fr Bernard was a monk in his fifties who had been at the monastery for twenty years. He had an exemplary record to date. Fr Bernard has been a priest for twenty years, and because of his low morale he never progressed to being chief abbot. He was very disaffected, but he kept this to himself so no-one knew about his feelings of disaffection. He came across as very pleasant to his fellow clergy.

Majid muses,"I would hardly have thought Fr Bernard was the culprit, but you never know. These are troubled times so anything is possible.''

Majid goes back to his room to contemplate the latest events. As he does so he looks out the window and sees the splendour of the sunset.

He notices a little spider crawling up the wall next to the window, whereupon its front legs stood in an offensive manner."It makes me think, ''ponders Majid.

''Maybe like the spider I should go on the offence'' he muses. That he does.

The next morning, he is up for early prayers which are 4.30am. He surveys his fellow monks deep in prayer, and thinks that there is a murderer here in their midst.

Instead of praying hard, Majid is thinking and probing his thoughts about the perpetrator.

''Amen," they all sing in chorus. Early morning prayers are over. They all bundle back to their rooms.

As Fr Bernard walks back, Majid notices he has dropped something out of his pocket; A vial. Unbeknownst to the others he picks up the vial.

Later in his room he smells it and it smells very weird.

''Could this be the poison?'' he wonders.

''Egads, what next?'' he thinks.

In the church, both men and women pray in the pews, but only men are allowed to be monks or priests. Nuns could come and pray, and there were still a number sheltering at the monastery. They would come and pray every day. One day Majid notices something odd about one of the nuns. She isn't dressed as the others even in these days of civil war.

Her habit is dragging along the floor and the head bonnet seems tighter than normal.

''Ummm, that looks very strange,'' Majid thinks. So as the nun is leaving the church last on this occasion, Majid decides to act on a hunch. Majid stands on the back of the habit which causes the whole garment to come down.

Normally this would not be enough to pull the cloak down but on this occasion, it is loosely attached.

''Kerplunk," as the vestments fall to the floor to the floor to reveal a man!

Majid notices no body or facial hair and they could easily pass for a woman. "My God", exclaims Majid. "Fellow monks...'' he extols in a desperate fashion.

All the monks turn around and the man starts running through the grounds of the abbey. The scene is chaotic.

The semi-naked man is running through the gardens and lots of monks are chasing after him.

Finally, he starts to scarper up one of the walls but Majid, being the fastest and most agile, manages to grab his undergarment and pull him to the ground.

Majid shouts '' Did you poison Fr Matthias?" A deep voice replies,'' I did it for the rebel cause''

Fr Matthias was secretly planning to kill the leader of the rebels by ingratiating himself with his adjutants.

''Fr Matthias was going to let in some of the rebels (this was a feint) at the front gate of the abbey, in exchange for giving the rebel leader confession, whereupon he would have stabbed our leader," states the rebel nun. ''He had to go."

The monks take the rebel male nun to a lockup at the abbey, where a guard is put on duty.

Meanwhile still gunfire and cannon fire can be heard in the distance.

Majid still wonders how Fr Bernard came into possession of the vial. Under investigation, the rebel nun reveals he had used a small bottle and not a vial, so this had exonerated Fr Bernard.

But it was still nagging him though, what the vial was for and why it was in his pocket.

''Ummmm, these are strange times,'' mused Majid.

CHAPTER 4

Meanwhile, back at James' place the nuns are cowering in the darkness at his house. After midnight one of the nuns, now normally dressed, sneaks out of the house.

It is pitch black outside and she is rushing down the road.

Back at the monastery the rebel male nun is demanding food.

''Give me some bread, you scoundrels,'' he yells at the monk guard. The monk guard pays no attention.

Majid is still musing about Fr Bernard and the vial. "A mystery," he ponders.

The nun from James' house has now reached the outer stairs of the secret passage into the abbey grounds via the gardens.

She struggles to push the door open but finally makes it. She rushes in and is looking for Majid. She finally finds Majid, who is near the rebel nun's cell.

She approaches as Majid is leaving the cell, and the rebel nun sees her.

''Don't listen to her,'' the rebel nun shouts. "Sister Helena, what are you doing here?'' Majid asks.

''I have come to warn you of impending destruction,'' she replies.

''The rebels have developed a latest potent destructive form of gunpowder,'' whispers Sr Helena.

''What!'' shouts Majid."'Yes, we have a traitor amongst us,'' replies the sister.

''Who?'' exclaims Majid. ''Don't listen to her, Majid,'' interjects the rebel nun from the cell.

''Who, Sr Helena?......I must know," retorts Majid.

''It is Fr Bernard who has defected to the rebel cause,'' replies the sister.

''Why?'' replies Majid.

''Fr Bernard wanted to destroy the order as he never became abbot, as he believed he should have,'' said Sr Helena. Sr Helena is a very erudite lady who has been so supportive to Majid, especially as he came from an impoverished background in Algeria. She is a person who is always willing to help.

So Majid went to confront Fr Bernard. He was in his room. Majid knocked on his door. ''Who's there?" shouts Fr Bernard.

''It is I," 'replies Majid.

Sensing that his time is up, Fr Bernard starts crawling through the open window. He cries back "won't be a moment.''

Majid has taken the master key and can open any room. ''Click."He gently opens the door.

He strains to see anything in the dark although he has his big candle.

He finds nothing, as the room is empty.

He rushes to the open window and looks out but sees only darkness. He has escaped.

''Darn,'' whispers Majid. "The vial that fell out of Fr Bernard's pocket could have something to do with a concoction related to new gunpowder," Majid wondered.

He goes back and alerts the other monks, and they form a search party. They strive into the night on a 'search and destroy' mission.

''The traitor must be found,'' shouts Majid.

''He has the explosive powder," he continues.

The party of six search for hours, but to no avail.

''Egads, where is the traitor?'' demands Majid.

Fr Bernard knows where Sr Helena is, and sneaks into the dormitory under cover of darkness.

He puts his hand over her mouth. Sr Helena is terrified. In the meantime, Majid and the gang are still searching.

Then a loud explosion is heard at the far left of the property, in the gardens where the priests march during Mass on feast days.

''Wow! Did you hear that, fellow monks?'' exclaims Majid.

Majid & the crew run towards where they heard the explosion.

They arrive and notice that the explosion was in the garden next to the wall, but it was not strong enough to breach the defences.

Meanwhile Fr Bernard, under cover of darkness, is taking Sr Helena down through the escape tunnel out of the abbey grounds.

Majid is closing in. The grounds are approximately 20 acres, so the search continues.

Majid sees a light in the distance, a candlelight near the escape tunnel out of the abbey.

He runs at fast pace as the light disappears down the tunnel.

He shouts "Give up Father!'' Fr Bernard reaches the exit and has a horse and cart ready to transport him away.

''Darn.'' cries Majid.

Sr Helena is in danger." Fr Bernard, who would have thought?'' shouts Majid. ''Ummmm,'' muses Majid.

He stares out across the river, contemplating his next move. He notices some ripples on the river. He looks closer, and notices some canoes in the darkness and then the canoes start to appear. ''Egads, it seems the rebels are planning an offensive from the river," he whispers to himself.

Majid locks the outer door of the escape tunnel and rushes back to the main buildings.

''Monks, we are about to be attacked from the water. Grab your guns!'' Majid shouts.

There is a flurry of manic activity. They must repel the threat.

Majid keeps most of the monks on the northern wall, but takes 20 to the southern sections to repel the water-borne invaders.

The monks take up their positions and there are slit holes to poke their guns through.

''Kabung,'' as one of the rebels fire upwards. The monks have their height advantage overlooking the river.

Then, 20 monks start firing back.

''Kabung! Kabung! Kabung!'' the shots ring out.

The rebels start falling back.

The river attack has been repelled.

Meanwhile Fr Bernard and Sr Helena reach the house where the other nuns are hiding. James peers through the slit in the curtains and sees some figures approaching in the darkness. The shadows are longer.

''Bang! Bang!'' resounds at the door.

Fr Bernard pushes Sr Helena through, with a pistol in her back.

''Oh my God!'' exclaims James.

The other nuns let out a scream.

Rebel gunfire can be heard but now much closer. ''Sr Helena was going to betray me," said Fr Bernard.

''I can't let that happen,'' he continues. "Right, you nuns come with me so I can get a good ransom from the rebels for you ladies,'' he states. The nuns gasp.

James' mind is working at lightening speed.

''What to do?" he ponders. James motions towards the door.

''What are you doing, James?'' shouts Fr Bernard.

''There is no getting away for you,'' he continues. In fact, James was thinking about getting his gun from the shed in the garden, but was wondering how to secure it.

Back at the monastery the water rebels are finally defeated and there is no breach of the monastery walls.

Majid's quick thinking avoided disaster.

''Ummm, what to do about Fr Bernard and Sr Helena?'' he ponders.

"I must get a search team together. I wonder if Fr Bernard went to James' house? He knows that James' house is often used as a refuge during troubled times". Meanwhile the rebel leader, Jose, has met with his bedraggled remaining water-borne troops at his camp.

''We were out-smarted and out-gunned,'' one of the rebels states.

''We have to think of new ways or bypass the monastery.'' Jose comments.

CHAPTER 5

Back at James' house, James sneaks out as Fr Bernard is distracted by one of the nuns. He goes to the shed and gets his gun.

Fr Bernard now realises James has disappeared and is worried, so he grabs Sr Helena and points the gun at her head whilst he stands at the window, and with the light on, they can be seen from the outside.

Fr Bernard yells out and says, ''Give yourself up James otherwise I will kill Sr Helena''.

The other nuns are cowering in the back except for Sr Simona, who has an idea.

She predicts James would have his gun by now. She decides to make a move.

Sr Simona rushes forward and pushes Fr Bernard, which knocks the gun out of his hand and at the same moment James fires his gun from outside, as he can sense he can achieve a clear shot.

''Bang! 'goes James' gun.

The shot hits Fr Bernard in the right shoulder, which sends him back with a jolt.

He collects himself and shuffles out the back door.

James comes back in the front door and comforts the other nuns. They are all crying, including Sr Helena.

Fr Bernard has escaped. He is bleeding profusely.

CHAPTER 6

Back at the monastery, although the sound of the gunfire is still heard in the distance, it is very muffled and quite sporadic.

Majid corrals his monk troops and gives them a pep talk. He still has guards on the walls of the abbey grounds. Life is slowly returning to some order, but still a long way from normal. Prayers are again at 5.00pm, with dinner at 7.30 for some of the monks.

Fr Bernard finally makes it to the rebel camp, but he is exhausted and has lost a lot of blood.

The rebel medics start patching him up immediately. He finally rests and falls asleep.

Jose stays up thinking of his next move. Morning comes as the 300 rebels are doing their exercises with their squad leaders.

Fr Bernard awakes late and has breakfast. Jose approaches and sits down with the monk, and they mull over tactics.

''Ok, let us attack on 3 fronts,'' says Fr Bernard.

''Do you think that will work with our exhausted troops?'' Jose asks.

''It is our best chance.'' the rebellious monk replies.

''Ok let's make plans,'' Jose exclaims. He has a long scar on his face similar to a monk who lived at the monastery 15 years ago but left the order disgruntled. He always harboured a grudge against the abbey when he left.

Back at the monastery Majid is working on a new project making ''hand grenades'' like gunpowder bombs.

He goes back to the cell where the 'rebel nun' is housed and interviews him again.

''What are the rebel plans?'' shouts Majid aggressively.

''I will never tell you even if I did know,'' he replies. ''What about the rebel leader? I heard he was an ex-monk at the abbey years ago." Majid continues.

''You have to work it out.'' said the bearded nun.

''He was a disenchanted, disgruntled monk.'' Majid replies.

''Well, your days are numbered," the hirsute rebel nun replies.

Jose and the squad leaders start marshalling their forces into 3 groups. The groups are now on the march. Jose is a leader of the rebels, and is working with other group across the country. It is a time of civil war and there is disruption everywhere. He has had an intense hatred for the monastery due mainly to his atheistic beliefs. He developed a friendship with Fr Bernard when they met by chance in a local village. Their joint project is to destroy the monastery.

In a few hours they will be at the monastery. They are on the move.

Jose is marshalling his forces. They are reaching the outskirts of the town. They are in their 3 groups; one to the north, and one to the south walls, and one to the west walls. East was the water-borne attack which failed.

Meanwhile Majid is visiting the wounded at the monastery. A makeshift medical unit with beds is set up in a large room near the common room. It is a cold place with a clinical look about it, appropriate for its new purpose. It has tall pillars in the coroners of the makeshift hospital. One of his clerical colleagues, Fr Wilson, has had medical experience before he joined the abbey. He was an army medic.

They are patched up the best he can do, and he treats the monks for all ailments. He has become especially busy during the civil war attacks treating injured monks.

Fr Wilson is currently working on a monk who is stronger now, enough to withstand removing a bullet from his right shoulder.

The fellow monk is laced with Benedictine liquor, and the same alcohol is dousing the wound. He bites onto a piece of wood.

Majid grits his teeth. He notices a fly crawling up the stained-glass pane window searching for deliverance or an opening to the outside world. The fly finds the exit. The bullet is removed.

Jose is at the approaches of the abbey.

He yells, ''God be with us.''

The rebel troops respond ''Yeha yeah.''

"Yehaaaaaa yehaaaa," as the rebel troops advance.

Majid Marshals his troops to the walls.

'Ye —-haaaa," he shouts.

Sr Helena is approaching the outskirts of the abbey out of the clutches of Fr Bernard.

''Ye-ha,'' she whispers to herself.

Majid is worried about the lethal form of gunpowder that the rebels have developed.

''We must deploy all the monks,'' shouts Majid.

Sr Helena keeps pounding on the door. No answer!

''Help!'' she shouts. Then suddenly Majid opens the door.

''At last!'' she whispers to Majid.

''What is the latest, Majid?'' Sr Helena inquires as they scurry along the narrow tunnel and then finally ascend the narrow steps to the opening in the garden.

It is a dark and foreboding night.

''We have all the monks guarding all the walls, but we are worried about the rebels deploying their new lethal gunpowder," Majid replies.

''Kaboom'' resounds in the distance.

Majid exclaims, 'What the hell is that?'' as he looks at Sr Helena.

Meanwhile Jose and his troops are at the walls on 3 fronts.

Jose is behind his troops near the west wall.

The loud explosion is one of their makeshift bombs going off near the west wall, but fortunately no damage is reported.

Majid whispers to Sr Helena, "I will gather 8 monks and do a circling manoeuvre behind the rebels." "I am estimating Jose is at the west wall Sr Helena,'' Majid muses.

Meanwhile behind Jose's command point, keeping up the rear, is Fr Bernard & a few rebel guards. He is compromised because of his impaired wound still healing but he is up for the fight.

Majid and his troops are nearing their position. One of Majids' monks walks on one of the crinkled leaves, and this disturbs Fr Bernard and the rebels.

They immediately turn around & spot the troops creeping up on them.

''Bang! Bang!'' the guns roar.

In a flash, the bulk of the rebels lie dead. Fr Bernard survives.

Majid grabs Fr Bernard by the scruff of the neck and says, "You must tell me the rebel plans."

Under intense pressure, Fr Bernard reveals the rebel plans.

"Approaching on 3 fronts," Fr Bernard replies.

"Where is that lethal gunpowder?" Majid pursues.

"We have the bulk of it here," Fr Bernard replies.

Majid's monks tie up Fr Bernard and march him to the back of the abbey.

"Kapow! Kapow!" the shots ring out.

It gets louder as the small troops approach the outside secret entrance to the abbey.

They mount the narrow stairs under darkness & quickly bolt the outside door behind them.

Majid quickly rallies the rest of the monks to build a credible defence against the rebels.

Majid deploys the lethal gunpowder to his monk troops on the wall defences against the rebels on 3 fronts.

Sr Helena rallies, ''Boy, are they in for a surprise!''

Rebels approach, and they have a new secret weapon. Aerial bombardment!. Jose launches a series of kites and floating contraptions carrying bombs. The knack is once lit, it needs to go over the walls otherwise it winds back onto the rebel side. Soon there are floats above the abbey grounds.

''Crack crack'' resounds out. Then ....'' kaboom! Kaboom!'' as the kites explode. Many more fly over the grounds, with more explosions, but they are too high up to cause any great impact; terrifying for the monk troops but not effective. A few fly backwards with the wind and cause more problems for Jose's men as some rebel troops are injured. The experiment is not going to plan.

Majids' monks are firing guns on 3 fronts. Jose and his rebels are pulling back.

CHAPTER 7

Sr Helena is in the infirmary looking after the injured monks. She glances over towards the back of the lean figure of Fr Bernard. ''What shall she do?'' she whispers under her breath. He is strapped to a bed with restraints, a prisoner. At that moment a fly buzzes overhead and lands on one of Fr Bernard's shackles. Sr Helena thinks the fly is free and carefree, unlike the shackled prisoner.

Sr Helena looks over towards Majid with almost a loving glint in her eye, if not at least one of admiration for his all his hard work and leadership.

Majid casts a discerning eye towards Fr Bernard. He lies asleep strapped to his bed. ''What secrets he must have! He was always ambitious but never got the top job!'' Majid contemplates.

Suddenly one of Fr Bernard eyes squints open as Majid is hovering over him.

''What are Joses' weak points?'' Majid shouts beratingly. Sr Helena glances over with a concerned look.

Fr Bernard lies motionless and speechless, as the infection from his shoulder wound takes hold of his wracked body. Majid walks away. He goes to the makeshift munitions room. Several monks there have made about 30 hand grenades.

''Good work men," he solemnly adds. Soldiers the monks have become.

They still, where possible, attend daily prayers, but this has fallen back a bit understandably due to the fighting, but it keeps them centred and focused in their activities. Their motto is 'work and pray, and pray and work'. Majid carefully gathers up a bundle of bombs in his cloak and goes to the walls to deploy them to the fighting monks.

Jose's rebels send a few more kite bombs over which explode uneventfully & noisily over the abbey grounds, releasing a flurry of feathery bits remnants of the kites.

New grenades in hand, the monks yell, '' ye-ha''. Over the wall a grenade flies & explodes in the rebel ranks with devastating results. Parts of rebels fly bloodily into the air.

Meanwhile back at the infirmary Fr Bernard is starting to stir more from his previously motionless comatose state. He looks up this time & sees Sr Helena hovering over his bedside.

''What do you want sister?'' Fr Bernard says enquiringly. "I need your help to stop Majid!'' she declares. ''What changed your mind?'' Fr Bernard asks.

'He is a megalomaniac and out of control!'' she replies.'' We must stop him, '' she continues. Another grenade bomb can be heard in the near distance, presumably near the abbey walls.

''What's your plan, sister?'' Fr Bernard enquires in an upbeat tone, as if magically all his injuries have disappeared. ''We must trick him into leaving the abbey and be captured by rebel forces,'' she continues. ''How do we do that?'' Fr Bernard asks. "Let me worry about that and I will use all my womanly wiles,'' she remarks. ''I need to squirrel you out and back to Jose,'' Sr Helena says. ''Yes, that's the tack,'' Fr Bernard replies.

Meanwhile Majid is supervising his fighting monks. They are fighting back with grenades and shots. Sr Helena is moving Fr Bernard out of the infirmary under cover of darkness. She wants to take him through the secret passage in the back garden, and then onto Jose. But also she has to lure Majid out so she can get Jose to capture him. This is an elaborate plot to capture Jose, and then turn the rebel attack on its head.

Fr Bernard is ushered down the tunnel, but flops halfway down due to his unhealed injuries. Sr Helena says, 'Wait here, Bernie, I will be back.'' Already Sr Helena has caught up with Majid at the infirmary.

"What the hell is going on? ...... and where is the traitor?'' Majid exclaims. ''Don't worry, I have a plan," Sr. Helena replies positively. She continues, ''I have discovered Fr Bernard's secret signalling techniques to Jose''.

Majid & Sr Helena approach the entrance of the secret tunnel. Majid waits outside.

Sr Helena is back with Fr Bernard. ''I have sent the signals,'' Sr Helena continues.

''Jose won't be long,'' Fr Bernard replies.

Majid now has several of his warring monks with him, but they are out of sight of Fr Bernard.

Sr Helena helps Fr Bernard to the outside of the entrance as they can hear footsteps in the darkness

Majid is creeping down the tunnel with his monk bodyguards. ''Ssshhh,'' he says as they approach the exit of the tunnel.

Jose is striding forward with several rebel bodyguards.

Majid looks out from the tunnel exit and sees a candlelight in the near distance. Fr Bernard is waving a lantern from left to right, his 'signalling' messages.

As Jose approaches closer, Majid and the monks prepare themselves.

Suddenly a grenade bomb explodes nearby.

Sr Helena falls back from the rippling waves of the explosion into the arms of the approaching Majid.

In the confusion, Fr Bernard escapes with Jose and the rebel guards back into the darkness. The trap fails.

''I am glad you are safe, Sr Helena,'' Majid exclaims. ''That was close,'' she replies.

''Aaah, best laid plans....." Majid extols.

They hurriedly slam shut the door of the tunnel exit, and make their way back up the tunnel. The monk guards follow them upwards back to the East Garden.

''Kapow! Kapow!" as shots ring out. The outside door of the tunnel is not fully shut and the rebels start firing, using the door as protection. One of the monk guards is hit and falls heavily as Majid pushes Sr Helena to the floor to shield her from the rebel shots. The other monk soldier is firing and manages to repel the rebels, and then slams the door very tightly shut.

Then Majid carries the wounded monk warrior to the infirmary where his fellow monks will look after him. He has had a lucky escape, with only a flesh wound as the bullet exited out of his left shoulder.

Sr Simona is in the infirmary as Majid brings in the wounded monk. She quickly moved to assist Majid with laying the monk onto the bed.

''Bloody rebels,'' murmurs Majid in a hushed tone so as not to disturb the other patients in the infirmary. More bangs can be heard beyond the abbey walls, and Majid wonders what Fr Bernard is up to.

CHAPTER 8

Fr Bernard and Jose are now back at their basecamp and are plotting new forays against the monks. The base camp is surrounded by trees and is well hidden from the outside world. A number of fire pits have been set up around the camp to feed the hungry rebel hordes. The kite bombs didn't work but there are other modes of flight to terrorize the monastery.

Meanwhile Sr Simona stares out of the infirmary window. She sees a large bird flying out over the river. A spider on the other side of the glass interrupts her vision. She glares back at the prostrate figures of the monk patients who are battling with their injuries. Majid walks in with Sr Helena, fresh from their explosive encounter with the rebel in the East Garden.

"Sr Simona, how are our patients doing?" Majid enquires. ''Slowly recovering, but it has been difficult. We really need a surgeon,'' Sr Simona replies.

Majid sees the same spider on the window but this time staggering down the pane somewhat erratically. Sr Helena looks on somewhat bemusedly.

Majid walks over and takes a closer look, whereupon at that instant a dozen or so flying insects hit the window and fall to the floor, which startles Majid.

''Ummmm, what could this be?'' muses Majid. Another bomb explodes, but this time it lands right in front of the church doors. ''It was dropped from above,'' screams one of the monk soldiers who comes dashing in with blood from a head wound.

''My God!'' says Majid.

''We need to investigate straight away'' shouts Sr Helena. The sisters and Majid run outside, following the bloody monk.

Majid looks up and sees large, winged beasts with what look like bombs in their claws, dropping their lethal packages in the abbey grounds.

''Quick quick........ my monk warriors, start shooting these beasts down,'' he shouts out.

The sisters are back inside the infirmary tending to the injured monks. The bloodied monk with the head wound is being wiped and bandaged by Sr Simona.

''Tink tink'' emanates from the window on the left. Sr Simona glances over at the window where the hapless spider was, and notices more insects are hitting the window and then dropping lifeless to the floor.

She frowns and ponders what is happening with this strange event, the likes of which she has never seen before.

Majid and Sr Helena also walk towards the window and notice the lifeless insects.

''Quick, quick sisters .... I have an idea,'' Majid states. ''Let us get these insects to the monk laboratory.'' he continues. Sisters Helena & Simona start gathering up the fallen insects.

Sr Helena looks up and sees a large bird carrying an object in its claws, seemingly heading for the infirmary.

''Majid, Majid!'' shouts Sr Helena, looking towards Majid.

Majid now notices the winged intruder heading on a trajectory right for them, and so he shouts, 'Hit the deck everyone, the bird is carrying a bomb." Mayhem and chaos ensue as patients are dragged from their beds to the floor, spilling blood over the shiny tiles as they have only seconds to spare.

Then, 'kaboom! Kaboom!'' as the bombs explode near the window spraying dust in all directions.

The monk scientists discover that the insects have a deadly toxin inside them, which if harnessed against the human population will cause devastation.

Majid says enquiringly of Fr Brittain, '' What is the progress on the dead insects?'' Fr Brittain is chief science monastic officer, and he is responsible for developing good cures, and also other things to assist with the defence of the monastery.

''We have isolated a toxin from the bugs which we have tested on grasshoppers, with immediate deadly results!'' Fr Brittain replies.

''Egads, this is a breakthrough!'' exclaims Majid. ''We will design it against the vulture bombers and rebels,'' Majid continues.

Sr Simona remarks, '' One of the monk patients has just died and he left with me with his final words.''

"Beware the skies!'' the dead monk had said.

Jose and Fr Bernard are now planning new tactics; a frontal assault on the monastery.

'' We will need all our troops ready for the frontal assault,'' extols Fr Bernard. Jose replies, '' Yes we will.".

''Get ready,'' they both exclaim.

Sr Helena, who is friendly with Fr Bernard, wants to go through the Northern Garden passage and listen into their plans.

Sr Helena recruits Sr Simona and off they go. Down the secret passage and out to the outside the sisters walk gingerly so as not to be heard. The sisters are creeping upon the rebel camp. They can hear the leaders plotting.

Fr Bernard says ''We will hit the front gate with all our troops.''

''Wow,'' whispers Sr Helena. ''We have the advantage now. We need to report back to Majid,'' whispers Sr Simona.

Meanwhile, Fr Brittain has produced some deadly toxin and has made 12 vials of the product.

''If we shoot the toxin at the vulture warriors then we will have the upper hand in the skies,'' contemplates Majid.

CHAPTER 9

Meanwhile, Fr Bernard and Jose are finalizing their frontal assault. They plan to release vulture bombers first, as a shock wave, and then follow up with rebel soldiers storming the front gate. ''That is an ingenious plan,'' proclaims Jose to Fr Bernard. ''We will have the abbey by nightfall'' Fr Bernard boasts.

''Fr Brittain, have we had sufficient toxic vials now?'' asks Majid. Fr Brittain retorts, '' all going to plan.''

Majid is now surveying the infirmary, looking at a dozen wounded monks. He doesn't notice the staring eyes of Sr Helena looking on intently.

It is now early morning, and Majid has had very little sleep as he trains his eyes on the cloudless skies. He ponders what might come from that direction today. The sky-blue contrasts with the darker blue of the river. He notices a spider on the window leaping and capturing a small insect and engulfing it in its web. But the insect wriggles free and manages to escape. He ruminates whether the monks are the small insects, and the spider represents the rebel cause. Majid's mind drifts as Sr Helena walks up behind and puts a reassuring hand on his hip which momentarily takes him back. All the injured monks are either in a coma or asleep.

''What are you thinking about?'' enquires Sr Helena. They don't realise that Sr Simona is peering at them from the other side of the room whilst tending to a patient.

''Ahh, the big day is today ....I can sense it,'' says Majid expectedly.

''Are we prepared, Majid?'' Sr Helena asks.

''We have 30 vials of toxin now produced by Fr Brittain and his team. And we have our warrior monks with our bomb grenades.'' Majid continues. ''Sounds good,'' Sr Helena replies.

Sr Simona knows from her eavesdropping scouting mission that the frontal assault will probably be today. She muses over the closeness of Majid and Sr Helena. She feels a pang of jealousy, which she tries to dismiss but finds it difficult. She wonders how close they have become. Is it sexual? But if so, when did they find the time? All these questions mull around in her mind.

''Kerpang! Kerpang! .... '' the church bells ring out for 9.00am Mass.

The remaining monks, minus the ones on guard duty, attend Mass. Sr Helena sits next to Majid whilst Sr Simona is 2 pews back watching the pair intently rather than thinking about the Mass. Sr Helena and Majid seem unusually close in the pews. Sr Simona looks around and wonders if anyone else notices what she can sense between them. ''I suppose war affects people in different ways,'' Sr Simona speculates. Halfway through church proceedings a large bang can be heard near the front gate. And then another bang and then another. The monks in church all pile out into the yard in front of the church entrance.

Majid sees vultures flying overhead dropping bombs, while one of the warrior monks on the wall yells, "Approaching rebels .... approaching rebels.".

Fr Brittain's toxic vials are now in the hands of the monk leaders. ''If the arrow doesn't kill the vultures, then the toxin will!'' shouts Majid.

''Look out Majid,'' Sr Helena shouts as a kite bomb drifts over the wall & into the monastery grounds. A monk soldier fires at the kite bomb and it explodes, spurting shrapnel all over his colleagues.

And Fr Bernard looks better than when he was shot, although he waddles with a limp now. Fr Bernard and Jose are 20 meters behind their troops.

''Jose, send me more vulture & kite bombs,'' shouts Fr Bernard.

"The vultures seem infected; they are frothing at the mouth,'' shouts Jose.

Majid and Sr Helena did indeed have an affair and produced a child 18 years ago, Michael, and he was fostered out.

What they don't know now is that he is returning as a rebel soldier, and is outside the gates. He never knew anything about his parents, except they were both in the clergy, and Majid and Sr Helena knew he had a red birthmark on his left neck.

CHAPTER 10

The rebels are attacking towards the front gates, and the monk warriors are firing from the walls.

Then, rebel troops with battering rams finally break through the front gate. Twenty rebel soldiers pile through, but Fr Brittain is ready for them. He has armed the second monk platoon with rifles filled with vials of toxin. They fire in unison. The first line of rebel soldiers falls down, frothing at the mouth.

Majid looks at Sr Helena with some psychic intuition about their wayward son. They know he is roughly 18 now, but after his birth he was taken to a foster house by Fr Bernard, as the orders couldn't tolerate sex within their religious institutions.

But they can sense that their son is nearby. They are not sure how or why. Majid gets a tingly sensation on the back of his neck, and Sr Helena has a gut feeling. What next?

A vulture bomb explodes over the church spire, and a fire breaks out. The third platoon of monk soldiers gather up pails of water to put the fire out. In the meantime, the second platoon of monk soldiers keep firing vials of toxin to halt the rebel advance. The first platoon has suffered badly and is retreating back to their peers. They have lost half their numbers.

Suddenly amidst the smoke, a tall blond strapping lad emerges behind the other troops, gesticulating towards his fellow soldiers. Definitely a leader in the making!

He can see the soldiers that are down and frothing at the mouth. He tries to corral his fellow soldiers and move towards the monk soldiers. There is chaos & mayhem.

Michael slowly looks up and catches the eye of Majid, just as a bomb explodes over Majid and Dr Helena. Splinters and shrapnel splat everywhere. A splinter hits Sr Helena in the head, and she falls to the ground, blood pouring out. Majid turns and rushes towards her.

Majid bends down and cradles Sr Helena in his arms. She is fading fast, and Majid is aware of nothing else but her slow deliberate breathing. He is not aware of the fighting and is completely focused. Her dying breaths are laboured and Majid is taking it all in. Michael rushes over and stands above Majid and Sr Helena. Majid looks up with tears in his eyes, and this causes a similar reaction with Michael. Majid recognizes his son from his distinctive birth mark, and more tears well up. He can hardly believe it.

More bombs explode around the trio, but they are all oblivious. Finally, Sr Helena takes her dying breaths. Majid and Michael are crying profusely. Majid carries her into the chapel and Michael assists.

The soldiers are still fighting, but the rebels have taken a battering from the toxin and the grenades, and they are now in full retreat.

Jose & Fr Bernards' plans have failed.

Printed in Great Britain
by Amazon

51088000R00027